The Celebrity Cookbook

Movie Meals, Silver Screen Suppers &
Tinseltown Treats

40 Favorite Foods & Recipes of the Rich &
Famous

BY

Stephanie Sharp

License Notes

My deepest thanks for buying my book! Now that you have made this investment in time and money, you are now eligible for free e-books on a weekly basis! Once you subscribe by filling in the box below with your email address, you will start to receive free and discounted book offers for unique and informative books. There is nothing more to do! A reminder email will be sent to you a few days before the promotion expires so you will never have to worry about missing out on this amazing deal. Enter your email address below to get started. Thanks again for your purchase!

Just visit the link or scan QR-code to get started!

https://stephanie-sharp.subscribemenow.com

Table of Contents

Introduction

The Celebrity Cookbook brings together the tastiest and most iconic dishes across the decades.

Not only family-friendly recipes including Dwayne (the Rock) Johnson's favorite pancakes and John Wayne's Cheese Casserole but also dinner-party gourmet meals to impress your friends.

Enjoy Nicole Kidman's Crispy Orecchiette with Broccoli, Pine Nuts & Parmesan or Leonardo DiCaprio's Kale, Ricotta and Cannelloni Pasta.

Discover 40 sweet and savory recipes brought to you by your favorite celebrities.

Now you too, with the help of the Celebrity Cookbook, can create movie star meals, silver screen suppers and Tinseltown treats.

If you are searching for a star-studded menu, then look no further than these 40 fabulous favorite recipes of the rich and famous.

Movie Meals & Silver Screen Suppers

Arnold Schwarzenegger: Burger

It stands to reason that any recipe courtesy of the former Governor of California would be beefy. You will love this Austrian-style burger.

Servings: 1

Total Time: 8hours 20mins

Ingredients:

- Cooking oil
- Jalapeno pepper (minced)
- 1 garlic clove (peeled, crushed)
- 1 small turkey steak
- Spiced mayonnaise
- Fresh ground horseradish
- 1 pumpkin kernel roll (halved)
- 1 slice Dachsteiner cheese
- Ketchup
- 2 slices of tomato
- 2-3 salad leaves
- 2-3 drop pumpkin seed oil

Directions:

1. In a shallow bowl mix sufficient the cooking oil, minced pepper, and garlic to marinade the turkey steak, and transfer to the fridge overnight.

2. The next day, mix mayonnaise with some ground horseradish. Cut the roll in half; toast it slightly. Cook the steak on stove top or grill until no pink remains.

3. Fill the roll with spiced mayonnaise, cheese, ketchup, turkey steak, spiced mayonnaise, tomato slices, salad leaves and a few drops of pumpkin seed oil.

Ben Stiller: Chicken Shawarma

In 2018, Ben Stiller, Hollywood superstar took on his role as a Goodwill Ambassador for the UN Refugee Agency. To mark World Refugee Day in June of that year, he got together with Ahmed Badr, a former Iraqi refugee, and writer. The pair came together in a film to create Chicken Shawarma, a traditional dish from the former refugee's home in Baghdad.

Servings: 4

Total Time: 2hours 10mins

Ingredients:

Chicken:

- 1 tsp ground cardamom
- 1 tsp cumin
- ½ tsp cinnamon
- 1 tbsp paprika
- 1 tsp garlic powder
- 1 tsp turmeric
- ¼ tsp cayenne
- 1 tbsp sumac
- 1 tsp fresh ground black pepper
- 1 tbsp kosher salt
- 4 tbsp olive oil
- 1 tbsp freshly squeezed lemon juice
- 3 cloves garlic (peeled, sliced)
- 2½ pounds skinless, boneless chicken thighs (trimmed)

White Sauce:

- 1 cup whole milk Greek yogurt
- 1 tbsp freshly squeezed lemon juice
- 1 clove garlic (peeled, minced)
- 1 tsp sumac
- ⅛ tsp cayenne pepper
- ¼ tsp salt
- ¼ tsp black pepper

To Serve:

- Pita bread (warm)
- Cucumber (thinly sliced)
- Tomato (sliced)
- Pickle

Directions:

1. To a large bowl, combine the cardamom, cumin, cinnamon, paprika, garlic powder, turmeric, cayenne, sumac, black pepper, kosher salt, oil, lemon juice, and garlic and whisk to combine.

2. Add the chicken thighs to the bowl and evenly coat.

3. Cover the bowl and chill in the fridge for between 1-12 hours.

4. Next, prepare the sauce: To a bowl, add the yogurt to the lemon juice, garlic, sumac, cayenne pepper, salt, and black pepper. Mix to combine and transfer to the fridge, to chill.

5. Position the oven rack approximately 6" from the top heat source in the main oven and preheat your grill.

6. Using aluminum foil, line a baking sheet and wire rack.

7. Arrange the chicken on the prepared rack in a single layer, with the smooth sides facing downwards. Grill until the chicken until browned and registering a minimum of 165 degrees F on an internal meat thermometer. This will take between 15-20 minutes. Rotate the grill halfway through.

8. Remove the chicken and set aside to rest for 4-6 minutes before handling.

9. Turn the oven off.

10. While the chicken is resting, warm the pita in the oven for 2 minutes.

11. Thinly slice the chicken into strips and serve with cucumber, tomatoes, pickles, homemade sauce and pita.

Brad Pitt: Make-Ahead Breakfast Casserole

This casserole is superstar Brad's mom's favorite recipe. Make ahead, and the following morning you will have a satisfying and comforting breakfast for your little A-listers.

Servings: 4-6

Total Time: 1hour

Ingredients:

- 1 pound mild pork sausage
- 6 eggs
- 2 cups milk
- 1 tsp dried mustard
- 1 tsp salt
- 2 cups bread cube crusts
- 8 ounces Cheddar cheese (shredded)

Directions:

1. Over low heat, in a frying pan, brown the sausage until no pink remains. Drain any excess grease and set to one side to cool.

2. In a bowl, lightly beat the eggs.

3. Add the milk, followed by the mustard and salt and mix well to combine.

4. Stir in the cubes of bread, add the cooked sausage along with the cheese, mixing to combine.

5. Transfer the mixture to a shallow casserole dish of 2-quart capacity and place in the fridge, overnight.

6. The following morning, remove the casserole dish from the fridge and preheat the main oven to 350 degrees F.

7. Bake the casserole in the oven for between 40-45 minutes, until the edges are golden. Serve hot.

Cary Grant: Mushroom Canapés

Next time you host a cocktail party wow your guests with these simple mushroom canapés courtesy of this suave and sophisticated forties superstar.

Servings: 4-8

Total Time: 6mins

Ingredients:

- 1 (8 ounce) can mushrooms (drained, chopped)
- 2 tbsp oil
- 1 cup spinach (chopped)
- 1 tomato (chopped)
- 1 tbsp French dressing
- 2 splashes Tabasco sauce
- 8 slices bread
- Butter

Directions:

1. In a pan, sauté the mushrooms in oil for 5 minutes, taking care not to brown.

2. In a bowl, combine the spinach and the tomato with the French dressing and Tabasco sauce.

3. Toast the bread until golden and butter one side.

4. Arrange the mushroom mixture on the buttered side of the toasted bread and serve.

Cate Blanchett: Goat Cheese Tart with Peaches

Cate Blanchett is no stranger to cooking. In fact, while in high school, she worked in the kitchen of an elderly care home. This deliciously sweet and savory appetizer or lite bite is said to be one of her favorites.

Servings: 6

Total Time: 35mins

Ingredients:

- Nonstick baking spray
- 1 (14 ounce) package frozen puff pastry (defrosted)
- 4 ounces goat's cheese (softened)
- 6 ripe, sweet peaches (peeled, pitted, cut into thin wedges)
- Freshly ground black pepper
- 2 tbsp runny honey

Directions:

1. Preheat the main oven to 400 degrees F. Line a baking sheet with aluminum foil. Lightly spritz the foil with nonstick cooking spray.

2. Cut the pastry into 6 (4") squares and arrange on the sheet.

3. With a fork, prick each square.

4. Spread a spoonful of cheese onto each square, allowing a thumbnail border.

5. Top each of the squares with peaches.

6. Bend the border upwards and season with a dash of pepper.

7. Bake in the oven for between 20-25 minutes rotating the pan halfway through baking until the pastry is golden and puffed and the peaches softened.

8. Remove from the oven and drizzle with honey.

Dame Helen Mirren: Cabbage Pies

Star of the silver screen, British actress Helen Mirren likes nothing more than to prepare this dish with sister, Kate. The cabbage pies are a homage to their Russian roots.

Servings: 2-4

Total Time: 55mins

Ingredients:

- 3 tbsp butter
- ½ cup chicken stock
- 1 medium white cabbage (thinly sliced)
- 2 leeks (thinly sliced)
- 1 medium onion (peeled, chopped)
- 2 store-bought, refrigerated pie crusts
- 3 tbsp parsley (chopped)
- 3 hard-boiled eggs (peeled, chopped)
- Milk (to brush)

Directions:

1. Preheat the main oven to 350 degrees F.

2. In a large frying pan, mix the butter with the stock over moderately low heat.

3. Add the cabbage, leeks, and onion and while occasionally stirring cook until the veggies are softened, and the cabbage is al dente, for approximately 10 minutes. When cooked remove from the heat and set aside to cool.

4. On a clean work surface, lightly dusted with flour, roll the pie crust out to a ¼ "thickness Cut out 6 circles and set to one side.

5. When the veggies are cooled, drain and transfer to a mixing bowl.

6. Add the parsley and the eggs before seasoning and stir to combine.

7. Add the veggies evenly to the center of the pastry circles. Brush the edges of the circles with a drop of milk and pinch together to seal.

8. Arrange the pies on a greased baking sheet brush the tops of the pies with milk and bake in the oven for between 20-25 minutes, until golden.

9. Serve and enjoy.

Elizabeth Taylor: Chicken with Avocado and Mushrooms

As much at home in the kitchen, as she was on set, we reveal screen goddess Elizabeth Taylor's signature dish.

Servings: 6-8

Total Time: 1hour 30mins

Ingredients:

- 1 tbsp freshly squeezed lemon juice
- 1 Hass avocado (peeled, pitted, cubed)
- Salt and freshly ground pepper
- 2 (2½ pound) chickens (cut into strips)
- ¼ cup butter
- Fresh parsley (chopped, to garnish)

Sauce:

- 3 shallots (finely chopped)
- 3 tbsp cognac
- ⅓ cup dry white wine
- 1 cup whipping cream
- 1 cup chicken stock
- 2 cups fresh mushrooms (sliced)
- 3 tbsp butter

Directions:

1. Drizzle the lemon juice over the avocado, cover and transfer to the fridge.

2. Season the chicken.

3. Over low heat in a large frying pan, heat between 3-4 tbsp of butter. Add the chicken to the pan and fry until the chicken juices run clear, this will take between 30-40 minutes. Add more butter as needed.

4. Transfer the chicken to a platter and with aluminum foil, loosely cover and place in an oven set at 300 degrees F, to keep warm.

5. In the meantime, prepare the sauce.

6. To the same pan, add the shallots and over moderate heat, cook while stirring and scraping the bottom and sides of the pan.

7. Add the cognac followed by the white wine and bring to boil until almost evaporated.

8. Pour in the cream and boil for an additional 5 minutes.

9. Add the chicken stock to the mixture and over moderate heat, cook, while constantly stirring, until thickened.

10. While the sauce is cooking, over high heat, sauté the mushrooms in butter.

11. Add the mushrooms along with the marinated avocado cubes and gently stir until combined.

12. Pour the sauce over the chicken and garnish with chopped parsley.

Emily Blunt: Chicken Noodle Soup

Actress Emily Blunt serves this soup, her signature dish, to husband John. The star of Mary Poppins enjoys cooking and is said to be a wonderful chef.

Servings: 4-6

Total Time: 3hours 20mins

Ingredients:

- 2 yellow onions (peeled)
- 5 skin-on, bone-in chicken legs and thighs
- 5 fresh thyme sprigs
- 2 tbsp olive oil
- Sea salt and black pepper
- 5 carrots (diced)
- 4 celery stalks (diced)
- 2 garlic cloves (peeled, finely diced)
- 2½ tbsp fresh ginger (peeled, diced)
- 4 ounces dry white wine
- 3½ pints low-sodium chicken broth
- 3 chicken stock cubes
- 2 tbsp store-bought BBQ sauce
- 1 bay leaf
- 1 pound extra-wide egg noodles

Directions:

1. Preheat the main oven to 400 degrees F.

2. Finely dice one of the onions and set to one side. Halve the remaining onions lengthwise, before cutting into half-moons.

3. Scatter the onion slices on a baking sheet. Arrange the chicken on top.

4. Arrange the sprigs of thyme around the chicken before brushing them with a drop of oil and seasoning. Bake in the oven for between 30-40 minutes.

5. Remove the chicken from the oven and put to one side to cool.

6. In a cast iron casserole dish, heat the remaining oil over moderate heat.

7. Add the reserved diced onion, along with the carrots and celery and while occasionally stirring, sweat for approximately 5 minutes. Season.

8. Add the garlic along with the ginger and cook while stirring for an additional 3-5 minutes.

9. Pour in the white wine and allow to cool for 3 minutes before adding the chicken broth and stock cubes, bring to boil before turning the heat down to maintain a low simmer.

10. Remove the skin from the chicken and shred.

11. Add the shredded meat to the soup along with the onions and juices from the baking sheet.

12. Stir in the BBQ sauce along with the bay leaf and 2-3 chicken leg bones, cover with a lid and on very low simmer cook for approximately 2 hours.

13. When the soup is ready, remove the dish from the heat, remove and discard the bones along with the bay leaf and set to one side.

14. In the meantime, bring a pot salted water to boil.

15. Add the noodle and cook according to the package instructions.

16. Drain and divide the noodles between the individual bowls.

17. Ladle the soup over the noodles and serve.

Ingrid Bergman: Trout with Cream Sauce

Multi-award winning Swedish actress Ingrid Bergman had an appetite for good food and reputedly always went back for second helpings. This recipe will have everyone coming back for more.

Servings: 4

Total Time: 45mins

Ingredients:

- 4 whole trout
- Salt and black pepper
- Freshly squeezed juice of 1 lemon
- 1 pint thin cream
- Breadcrumbs
- Garnish:
- Lemon slices (to garnish)
- Parsley (chopped, to garnish)
- Tomato wedges (to serve)

Directions:

1. Arrange the trout in a heatproof casserole dish.

2. Season with salt and pepper.

3. Combine the lemon juice with 4 tablespoons of water and pour over the fish.

4. Transfer to the oven and bake at 350 degrees F for 20-25 minutes, until the fish flakes easily when using a fork.

5. Remove the trout from the casserole dish and pour the cooking liquor into a small pan.

6. Add the cream to the pan and by cooking over very high heat, reduce by half.

7. Return the trout to the casserole dish and pour the cream mixture over the top.

8. Scatter the breadcrumbs over the top and return to the oven to brown.

9. Serve garnished with slices of lemon, chopped parsley, and tomato wedges.

Jennifer Aniston: Skinny Pasta Carbonara

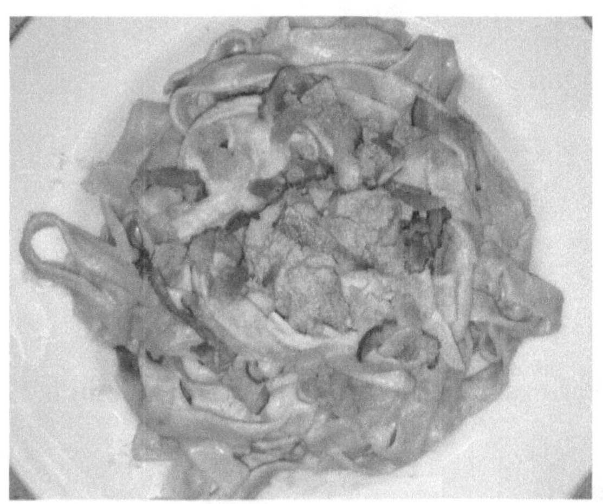

Jennifer Aniston and husband Justin Theroux admit to making this delicious carbonara every two to three weeks. Enjoy this gluten-free pasta dish with low-fat milk for a guilt-free Carbonara a la J & J.

Servings: 4

Total Time: 25mins

Ingredients:

- 1 pound gluten-free spaghetti
- 4 slices turkey bacon (diced)
- 1 red onion (peeled, diced)
- 2 garlic cloves (peeled, minced)
- 1 organic egg
- ⅓ cup skim milk
- ⅓ cup Parmesan cheese (freshly grated)
- Salt and black pepper
- Parmesan cheese (grated, to serve, optional)

Directions:

1. In a large pan of boiling salty water, start to cook the spaghetti until al dente. When sufficiently cooked set ¾ of a cup of cooking water to one side and drain the remainder.

2. In the meantime, over moderate heat, in a frying pan, fry the turkey bacon and onion for several minutes, until the onions are beginning to caramelize and the bacon is crisp.

3. Add the garlic, stirring frying until fragrant for 60 seconds. Remove the pan from the heat

4. Add the drained pasta to the pan containing the turkey bacon.

5. In a mixing bowl, whisk the egg with the milk and cheese.

6. Add approximately ½ cup of the cooking water, continually whisking to prevent the egg from becoming scrambled.

7. Pour the egg mixture into the pan with the pasta and toss to coat evenly. Adding additional water if needed.

8. Turn the heat to moderately low and cook for 60 seconds, until the sauce thickens.

9. Season to taste.

10. Remove from the heat and serve with additional Parmesan.

Jennifer Lopez: Ceviche

J-Lo's unprocessed diet is the secret to her body-beautiful, and she loves this sea bass ceviche appetizer/lite bite made with fresh and healthy ingredients.

Servings: 6

Total Time: 2hours 20mins

Ingredients:

- 1 pound sea bass (cut into small bite-sized cubes)
- 1 cup corn kernels (cooked)
- ½ cup green apple (cored, chopped)
- 1 tbsp red onion (chopped)
- Zest and juice of 2 fresh limes
- ½ tbsp extra-virgin olive oil
- 1 tbsp chives
- 1 tbsp plus Roma tomatoes (seeded, diced)
- ½ tsp kosher salt
- 1 cup cilantro (chopped, to serve)

Directions:

1. In a large bowl, combine the sea bass with the corn kernels, apple, onion, lime zest, lime juice, oil, chives, tomatoes, and salts.

2. Transfer to the fridge for a minimum of 2 hours, to marinate.

3. Garnish with chopped cilantro and serve.

John Wayne: Cheese Casserole

A big man with a big appetite, the Duke is said to have been a huge fan of this hearty, rich cheesy casserole. Be warned though, with two pounds of cheese, a little goes a long way!

Servings: 8

Total Time: 1hour 10mins

Ingredients:

- ⅔ cup canned evaporated milk
- 1 tbsp flour
- 4 egg yolks
- ½ tsp salt
- ⅛ teaspoon pepper
- 4 egg whites
- 1 tsp butter (to grease)
- 1 pound Cheddar cheese (grated)
- 1 pound Monterey Jack cheese (grated)
- 2 (4 ounce) cans diced green chiles (drained)
- 2 medium tomatoes (sliced)

Directions:

1. Preheat the main oven to 325 degrees F.

2. In a bowl, beat the milk with the flour and egg yolks. Season.

3. Beat the egg whites until stiff and gently fold them into the flour-yolks.

4. In a buttered casserole dish, combine the grated cheeses with the chiles.

5. Pour the egg mixture over the cheese and using a fork, ooze it through.

6. Bake the casserole in the oven and cook for 30 minutes.

7. Remove from the oven and garnish with tomato slices.

8. Return to the oven and bake for an additional 30 minutes.

Lady Gaga: Fried Turkey

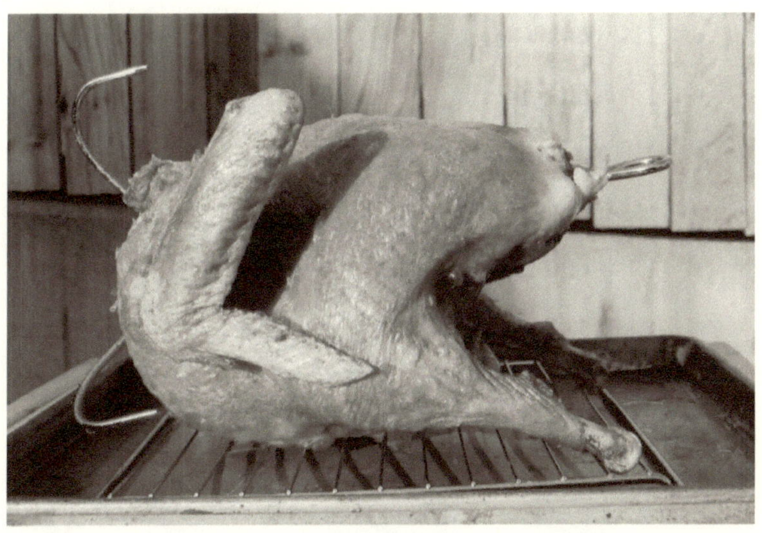

Singer-songwriter Lady Gaga recently featured in the 2018 version of A Star is Born, the unconventional celebrity enjoys nothing more than a home-cooked deep-fried turkey fragranced with herbs.

Servings: 6

Total Time: 50mins

Ingredients:

- 1 (10-12 pound) whole turkey
- 1½ tsp dry sage
- 1½ tsp thyme
- 1½ tsp Italian parsley
- 1½ tsp garlic powder
- 1 tsp onion powder
- 1 tsp salt
- 1 tsp black pepper
- 12 quarts peanut oil (to fry)

Directions:

1. Preheat the oil to 375 degrees F.

2. Remove the giblets along with the turkey's neck and discard.

3. Pat the turkey dry with kitchen paper towels.

4. Combine the sage, thyme parsley, garlic powder, onion powder, salt, and pepper.

5. Rub the turkey all over with the herb mix.

6. Place the turkey, breast side facing upwards in the fryer basket and gently and carefully lower the fryer basket into the hot oil while taking care not to splash any hot oil. It is important to maintain the oil temperature at 350 degrees F.

7. Fry the turkey for 3½ minutes/pound. Do not open the fryer until the frying time has expired.

8. Remove the oil to check that the turkey is sufficiently cooked and insert a meat thermometer not touching the bone into the thickest part of the turkey' thigh. The bird is cooked when the thermometer registers 180 degrees F.

9. Remove the turkey from the fryer, transfer to a chopping board and carve.

Leonardo DiCaprio: Kale, Ricotta, and Cannelloni Pasta

Taking inspiration from his Italian roots is this creamy cannelloni pasta dish, which you too, can now enjoy.

Servings: 2

Total Time: 1hour

Ingredients:

- 12¼ ounces butternut squash
- 6 cloves garlic (peeled, grated)
- 1 pound 6 ounces tomatoes (peeled, cubed)
- Salt and black pepper
- 7 ounces kale (chopped, rinsed)
- 7 ounces spinach (chopped, rinsed)
- 5¼ ounces ricotta cheese (grated)
- 1¾ ounces crème fraiche
- ¼ tsp nutmeg
- 8¾ ounces cannelloni tubes
- 1¾ ounces Parmesan cheese (grated)
- 1¾ ounces breadcrumbs

Directions:

1. Preheat the main oven to 360 degrees F.

2. In a pan, boil the butternut squash along with the garlic and tomatoes until softened. Drain and mash.

3. Add 2 cups of water to the butternut mixture.

4. Season the kale and spinach and cook until softened, for 8 minutes. Set aside to cool before stirring in the ricotta cheese, crème fraiche, and nutmeg.

5. Grease a 6" casserole dish with olive oil.

6. Spoon approximately half of the butternut sauce into the bottom of the dish.

7. Arrange the pasta tubes, standing upright in the sauce, making sure they are stable.

8. With a teaspoon fill each of the tubes 75 percent full with the kale-cheese mixture. Top up with the remaining pumpkins sauce.

9. Garnish with Parmesan and breadcrumbs and bake in the preheated oven for 25 minutes.

10. Serve immediately.

Liam Neeson: Glens of Antrim Stew

Born in Northern Ireland and proud of his roots, this authentic stew is said to be one of Liam Nesson's favorite dishes.

Servings: 4

Total Time: 1hour 45mins

Ingredients:

- 1 ounce butter
- 2 pounds lamb (cut into cubes)
- 1 yellow onion (peeled, chopped)
- 2 carrots (chopped)
- 1 tbsp plain flour
- 2 tbsp tomato puree
- ½ pint beef stock
- ½ tbsp sugar
- 2 potatoes (cut into cubes)
- 1 (11.2 ounce) bottle Irish stout
- 1 bouquet garni
- Salt and freshly ground black pepper
- Tabasco sauce

Directions:

1. In a pan, melt the butter.

2. In batches, add the meat to the pan and brown on all sides.

3. Remove the meat from the pan and add the onion along with the carrots, cooking until just softened.

4. Return the meat to the pan and stir in the flour followed by the tomato puree, stock, and sugar. Bring to boil before reducing to a simmer.

5. Add the potatoes along with the Irish stout, bouquet garni and salt, and pepper to taste.

6. Over low heat, cook for between 1½ hours until the meat is fork tender.

7. While the stew simmers, add between 4-5 drops of Tabasco sauce, to taste.

8. Serve.

Liv Tyler: Prawn Dumplings

Daughter of rock star Steve Tyler and best known for her role as Arwen Undómiel in the 2001 Lord of the Rings trilogy, Liv Tyler shares her love of Asian food.

Servings: 6

Total Time: 1hour 30mins

Ingredients:

Dough:

- 8¾ ounces dumpling flour + additional for dusting and cooking
- ½ cup warm water

Filling:

- 10½ ounces raw peeled king prawns (deveined)
- 1 (5 ounce) can water chestnuts (drained)
- 1" piece of fresh ginger (peeled)
- 6 spring onions (trimmed, finely chopped)
- 1 large egg (beaten)
- Sea salt
- ¼ tsp ground white pepper
- 1 tsp Shaoxing wine
- Sesame oil
- Vegetable oil

To Serve:

- Black rice vinegar
- Chili oil
- Sweet chili sauce
- Low-salt soy sauce

Directions:

1. To prepare the dough: In a bowl, gradually combine the flour with warm water, to form a ball.

2. On a lightly floured clean work surface, knead the dough until smooth for 5 minutes. Wrap the dough in kitchen wrap and set aside to rest for 30 minutes.

3. In the meantime, make the filling: Chop ⅔ of the prawn into 1/3" cubes. Finally, chop the remaining third and place in a bowl.

4. Peel the water chestnuts along with the ginger and finely chop.

5. Add the water chestnuts, ginger and spring onions to the bowl and add the beaten egg followed by a pinch of sea salt, white pepper, rice wine, and sesame oil, mixing well to combine.

6. On a clean work surface, lightly dusted work surface knead the dough a few times before cutting in half.

7. With a clean damp towel cover half of the dough.

8. Roll the remaining half of dough into a sausage shape approximately 16" long.

9. Break off ½ pieces and roll each one into a ball, before flattening into a 3" circle, approximately ¾" thick.

10. With a pastry brush, brush the edges of each circle with a drop of water.

11. Add 1 tbsp of the filling into the middle of each circle.

12. Fold the dough in half over the filling, and cup your hands around to seal and remove air bubbles. Make the pastry edges wavy and arrange the dumplings on a lightly floured platter.

13. When you are ready to cook the dumplings, place a large skillet or frying pan on moderate heat. Add 1 tbsp oil to the pan and heat.

14. In batches, fry the dumplings until the bottoms are golden.

15. In the meantime, whisk 4 tsp of flour with 3⅓ cups of water, re-whisking between batches. As soon as the bottoms of the dumplings are golden, pour in sufficient floury water to come ⅓" up the side of the pan.

16. Cover the pan with a well-fitting lid and simmer for approximately 5 minutes, before removing the lid until it starts to fry once more. You will see a pancake beginning to form and encase the dumplings. Once is golden, upside down, bang it out onto a chopping board.

17. Repeat the process with the remaining dumplings and flour water.

18. Prepare the dipping sauce by using the suggested condiments.

19. Serve.

Madonna: Burrito

Featuring in more than 25 movies, when it's time for a treat, this material girl likes nothing more than a Tex-Mex burrito.

Servings: 1-2

Total Time: 10mins

Ingredients:

- ½ cup cooked green lentils
- 1 tsp sesame oil
- 8 cooked green beans
- ½ cup carrot (cut into matchsticks)
- Pinch of sea salt
- 2 tortillas
- ¼ cup vegan mayonnaise
- 1 cup mixed salad greens
- ¼ cup sauerkraut
- ½ ripe avocado (peeled, pitted, sliced)

Directions:

1. Over moderately low heat, add the lentils to a pan with sufficient water to cover the bottom of the pan. Slowly warm, while continually stirring and set to one side.

2. In a second pan, over moderate heat, heat the sesame oil.

3. Add the green beans, carrots, and salt and sauté for 2-3 minutes. You may add between 1-2 tbsp of water if necessary. Set to one side.

4. Warm the tortillas in a toaster.

5. When toasted, evenly spread the mayonnaise on both tortillas.

6. Fill with mixed salad green, carrots, green beans, sauerkraut, avocado, and cooked lentils.

7. Roll into a burrito shape and enjoy.

Nicole Kidman: Crispy Orecchiette with Broccoli, Pine Nuts & Parmesan

Although Nicole Kidman admits to not being as good a cook as her two daughters, we have it on good authority this one her favorite pasta dishes.

Servings: 4

Total Time: 25mins

Ingredients:

- 1 pound orecchiette
- ½ cup vegetable oil (divided)
- 12 ounces broccoli florets
- 2 cloves garlic (peeled, slivered)
- ¼ cup dry white wine
- 3 tbsp freshly squeezed lemon juice
- Salt and black pepper
- 2 tbsp balsamic vinegar
- 3 tbsp butter (cut into chunks)
- ½ cup toasted pine nuts
- 2 ounces Parmesan cheese (freshly grated, divided)

Directions:

1. Cook the orecchiette according to the package instructions, Drain and rinse.

2. In a 12" frying pan or skillet, heat 3 tbsp of oil over moderately high heat until the pan is really hot.

3. Add half of the drained pasta and sauté until medium brown on the outside, for a few minutes. Do not touch the pasta while it develops its crispy, golden crust. Stir, and then cook until the same on the other side. Using a slotted spoon transfer the browned pasta to a pot.

4. Repeat the process with the remaining pasta along with 3 tbsp of oil.

5. Cover the pot to keep warm.

6. In the same skillet, heat the remaining oil on moderate heat.

7. Add the broccoli florets along with the garlic and while continually stirring cook for 5 minutes.

8. Pour in the wine and add the lemon juice followed by ¼ tsp salt and ⅛ tsp of black pepper.

9. Cook for 2-3 minutes until the broccoli is tender and crisp.

10. Add the broccoli mixture followed by the balsamic vinegar, butter, and pine nuts to the pasta in the pot and on moderate heat toss well until the butter entirely melts.

11. Add 1 ounce of Parmesan and toss to combine evenly.

12. Divide into 4 bowls and serve with the remaining grated cheese.

Reese Witherspoon: Shrimp and Grits

Growing up in Tennessee, Reese Witherspoon loves sharing the joys of good ole Southern cuisine, and it doesn't get much better than this classic coastal dish.

Servings: 6-8

Total Time: 45mins

Ingredients:

Grits:

- 1½ cups stone-ground grits
- 1 tsp salt
- 4 tbsp butter

Shrimp:

- 2 tbsp olive oil
- 1 tbsp butter
- 1 medium onion (peeled, chopped)
- 1 small green pepper (chopped)
- 3 cloves garlic (peeled, minced)
- 1 (14 ounce) can diced tomatoes + juice
- 1 tsp Cajun seasoning
- 2 tbsp tomato paste
- 2 pounds medium-large raw shrimp (peeled, deveined)
- ½ cup water
- 2 tsp Worcestershire sauce
- Salt (to taste)

- Chopped fresh green onions (to garnish)

Directions:

1. First, make the grits: In a pan over high heat, bring 3 cups of water to boil. Stir in the grits along with the salt and return to boil while occasionally stirring.

2. Reduce heat to low and stir in the butter, simmer for approximately 15 minutes. You will need to occasionally stir and add more water if needed to prevent them from becoming too thick.

3. Keep warm over low heat, adding additional water as needed and stirring once or twice to avoid them sticking or clumping.

4. To prepare the shrimp, over moderately high heat in a large frying pan, combine the oil with the butter.

5. When the butter is melted, add the onion along with the green pepper and sauté for 4 minutes, until just softened.

6. Add the garlic and cook for 60 seconds before stirring in the canned diced tomatoes along with their juices. Add the Cajun seasoning along with the tomato paste and stir to combine. Cook for 2-3 minutes.

7. Add the shrimp and stir for a couple of minutes, until the shrimp become pink.

8. Pour in the water and add the Worcestershire sauce, cooking for 2-3 minutes until not boiling but heated through.

9. Taste and adjust the seasoning.

10. Serve the shrimp over the grits and garnish with green onions.

Sophia Loren: Spaghetti with Tomato Sauce

Star of the silver screen, sexy Roman siren Sophia Loren shares her cherished spaghetti recipe. Sophia loved Italian food and when you prepare this simple pasta dish, you will too.

Servings: 6

Total Time: 30mins

Ingredients:

- Olive oil
- 3 cloves of garlic (peeled)
- 1 pound 2 ounces fresh tomatoes (peeled, seeded)
- Basil
- Pinch of salt
- 1 tbsp sugar
- 1½ pounds spaghetti
- Parmesan cheese (freshly grated)

Directions:

1. Over high heat, add a splash of oil to a large pan.

2. As soon as the oil begins to sizzle, add the garlic and sauté until lightly browned.

3. Next, add the tomatoes, along with a little basil and a liberal pinch of salt. Stir well to incorporate. Add 1 tbsp sugar and stir to combine.

4. Turn the heat down and simmer for 30 minutes.

5. After 15 minutes, and while the sauce simmers, prepare the pasta, cook the spaghetti in boiling salted water until al dente, drain.

6. Add the tomato sauce to the drained pasta, stirring to coat evenly.

7. Garnish with freshly grated Parmesan cheese and serve.

Tinseltown Treats

Anne Hathaway: Stuffed Peaches

It's no surprise that juicy ripe peaches stuffed with amaretti cookies and chopped almonds baked to peachy perfection is the dessert of choice for one of the world's highest-paid actresses.

Servings: 6

Total Time: 30mins

Ingredients:

- 3 large ripe peaches (pitted)
- 4 tbsp butter (divided)
- 2 tbsp. packed brown sugar (divided)
- 1 large egg
- ¾ cup amaretti cookies (coarsely crushed)
- 2 tbsp amaretto
- 1 tbsp almonds (finely chopped)
- Cream (to serve, optional)

Directions:

1. Preheat the main oven to 350 degrees F.

2. Scoop out and reserve half of the flesh from each of the peach halves.

3. Grease a ceramic baking dish with 1 tbsp of butter.

4. Arrange the peaches, so the hollow side is facing upward in the baking dish.

5. Chop the reserved peach flesh.

6. Combine 2 tbsp of butter with 1 tbsp of brown sugar and add to peach flesh.

7. Stir in the egg followed by the crushed cookies, and amaretto and spoon the mixture evenly into the peach halves.

8. Divide remaining 1 tbsp of butter into 6 portions and place one portion on each of the stuffed peaches.

9. Sprinkle peaches with chopped almonds and the remaining brown sugar.

10. Bake in the preheated oven for between 25-30 minutes, until peaches are softened and the topping is gently browned.

11. Serve with cream.

Barbra Streisand: Coffee Ice-Cream

This recipe has been doing the rounds for half a decade and is as good today as it was back then. Serve a la Streisand with crunchy pretzels.

Servings: 2-4

Total Time: 2hours 20mins

Ingredients:

- 1 cup whole milk
- 24 marshmallows
- 2 tsp instant coffee
- Pinch of salt
- 1 cup double cream (chilled)
- Pretzels (to serve)

Directions:

1. Set your fridge to its coldest setting.

2. Add the milk to a pan and heat. Add the marshmallows, 2-3 at a time and stir until the marshmallows are entirely melted.

3. Add the instant coffee along with a pinch of salt, stir to combine. Set the mixture aside to cool.

4. Whip the cream and fold it into the now cooled marshmallow mixture.

5. Pour the mixture into a freezing tray and transfer to the freezer to firm, approximately 2 hours.

6. Serve with pretzels and enjoy.

Cameron Diaz: Pumpkin Cupcakes with Chocolate Avocado Frosting

Cameron Diaz is all about longevity. She believes in living and eating well, and these flourless pumpkin cupcakes are the epitome of a healthy yet tasty treat.

Servings: 6

Total Time: 40mins

Ingredients:

- ½ cup pumpkin puree
- ½ cup natural peanut butter
- ⅛ cup honey
- 1 medium egg
- ½ tbsp molasses
- ¾ tsp baking powder
- ¼ tsp baking soda
- 1 tsp pure vanilla essence
- ½ tsp cinnamon
- ½ tsp ground ginger
- ⅛ tsp nutmeg
- ⅛ tsp cloves
- ⅛ tsp cardamom

Frosting:

- ½ large, ripe avocado (peeled, pitted)
- ⅛ cup cocoa powder
- 2 tbsp honey
- 1 tsp vanilla extract

Directions:

1. Preheat the main oven to 350 degrees F. Lightly grease a regular size 6-cup muffin pan.

2. Add the pumpkin puree, peanut butter, honey, egg, molasses, baking powder, baking soda, vanilla essence, cinnamon, ground ginger, nutmeg, cloves and cardamom to a food blender and process.

3. Divide the flourless batter between the 6 cups and bake in the oven for 20-25 minutes, until springy to the touch.

4. Set the cupcakes to one side to cool, while you prepare the frosting.

5. In a food blender, combine the avocado, with the cocoa powder, honey and vanilla extract and process until smooth. Transfer to the fridge until you are ready to frost the cakes.

Dame Judi Dench: Mini Cherry Bakewells

You don't have to be a dame to wow your guests with these delicious cherry bakewells.

Servings: 12

Total Time: 30mins

Ingredients:

- 1 (14 ounce) pack shortcrust pastry
- Plain flour (to dust)

Filling:

- ⅓ cup butter
- ⅓ cup caster sugar
- 1 large egg (beaten)
- 2½ ounces ground almonds
- Zest of ½ a lemon
- ½ tsp almond essence
- 1 heaped tbsp plain flour
- 4 tbsp Morello cherry jam

Topping:

- 4½ ounces icing sugar (sifted)
- 12 fresh cherries

Directions:

1. Roll the pastry out onto a lightly floured, clean work surface.

2. Cut the pastry into 12 (3½") circles.

3. Line a 12-cup muffin pan with the pastry circles and transfer to the fridge to firm, for half an hour.

4. Preheat the main oven to 400 degrees F.

5. To prepare the filling, in a bowl, beat the butter together with the sugar, egg, almonds, lemon zest, almond essence, and flour, until incorporated.

6. Evenly divide the cherry jam between the pastry cases.

7. Top with the almond filling and smooth the surface.

8. Bake in the preheated oven for between 18-20 minutes, until just golden, risen and springy to the touch.

9. Remove from the muffin pan and allow to cool on wire baking racks.

10. In a bowl, mix the icing sugar with sufficient water to make a runny, slightly thickened icing.

11. Spoon the icing over the now cooled tarts, allowing it to drizzle down the sides.

12. Add a cherry to the top of each tart and put to one side to set before enjoying.

Dwayne the Rock Johnson: Rock Bottom Pancakes with Banana

The Rock eats up to seven meals a day, and his fluffy and light world-famous pancakes are his go-to sweet treat.

Servings: 4-6

Total Time: 35mins

Ingredients:

- 1¼ cups flour
- 2 tbsp sugar
- 2 tsp baking powder
- ½ tsp salt
- 1 egg (beaten)
- 1 cup whole milk
- 1 tbsp cooking oil
- 2 bananas (to serve)

Directions:

1. In a bowl, combine the flour with the sugar, baking powder, and salt.

2. In a second bowl, combine the egg with the milk and cooking oil. Stir and add to the flour-salt mixture, stirring until slightly lumpy but blended.

3. For a regular size pancake, pour approximately ¼ cup of the batter onto a lightly greased hot skillet.

4. Cook the pancakes until golden, and bubbly before flipping them over and repeating the process.

5. Peel the bananas and cut into ¼" slices.

6. Place the slices of bananas between the layers of the golden pancakes and serve.

Eva Longoria: Cream Cheese Frosted Carrot Cake

Desperate housewife transformed into a domestic goddess, thanks to her Mom's delicious carrot cake with cream cheese frosting.

Servings: 8-10

Total Time: 1hour 30mins

Ingredients:

Cake:

- 2 cup all-purpose flour
- 1 tbsp ground cinnamon
- 2 tsp baking powder
- 1 tsp baking soda
- 1 tsp salt
- 1½ cups vegetable oil
- 2 cups sugar
- 4 large eggs (lightly beaten)
- 3 cups carrots (peeled, grated)

Cream Cheese Frosting:

- 1 pound cream cheese (room temperature)
- 1 cup unsalted butter
- 1 pound confectioner's sugar
- 2 tsp vanilla essence

Directions:

1. Preheat the main oven to 350 degrees. Grease and line 2 (9") cake pans.

2. In a bowl, sift the flour with the cinnamon, powder, soda, and salt.

3. In a second bowl beat the oil and sugar. Add the eggs, beating until incorporated.

4. Add the flour mixture to the wet ingredients, stirring until just blended.

5. In batches, add the carrots, gently folding to combine.

6. Transfer the batter into the prepared pans and bake for approximately 45 minutes, until browned and springy to the touch.

7. Allow the cakes to cook while still in the pans for 5 minutes, before removing from the pans and setting aside right side facing upward on wire baking racks.

8. In the meantime, and while the cakes cool, prepare the frosting.

9. In a bowl, beat the cream cheese with the butter until light and fluffy.

10. One cup at a time, add the confectioner's sugar, blending well between additions.

11. Fold in the vanilla and beat for 3-5 minutes, until silky smooth.

12. Spread the frosting all over the top and sides of the cake.

13. Enjoy.

Frank Sinatra: Lemon Ricotta Torte

Old blue eyes' favorite Italian dessert, this lemon ricotta torte is light and luscious.

Servings: 12

Total Time: 4hours 15mins

Ingredients:

- 3 pounds whole milk ricotta cheese
- 1⅔ cups sugar
- 4 medium eggs
- ½ tsp vanilla essence
- Zest from 1 fresh lemon
- Butter (to grease)
- Flour (to dust)

Directions:

1. Preheat the main oven to 400 degrees F.

2. In a bowl, mix the ricotta with the sugar, eggs, vanilla, and lemon zest until entirely combined.

3. Lightly grease and flour a 9x2" round baking pan.

4. Transfer the ricotta mixture into the pan and using a spatula, evenly spread.

5. Using aluminum foil, wrap a collar around the baking pan, to a minimum of 2" above the pan's rim. Secure the collar with either string or tape. The inside of the collar will need to be lightly greased.

6. Transfer to the preheated oven and bake on the bottom shelf for 55 minutes.

7. Set aside to cool.

8. When cool, place in the fridge for 3-4 hours.

9. Remove from the fridge and set aside until room temperature.

10. Serve and enjoy.

Gérard Depardieu: Rum Baba with Crystallized Pineapple

The French actor admits to having a penchant for fruity, juicy tarts and despite not being keen on all things sweet he enjoys a good dessert.

Servings: 4

Total Time: 2hours 30mins

Ingredients:

- 3½ ounces raisins
- 6¾ ounces aged rum
- 1⅓ tbsp fresh yeast
- 2 tbsp warm water
- 7 ounces sifted plain flour
- 2 tbsp caster sugar
- Salt
- 4 medium eggs (divided)
- 3½ ounces butter (softened)
- Syrup:
- 3⅓ ounces water
- 17½ ounces sugar
- Zest of 1 orange
- Zest of 1 lemon
- 1 vanilla pod
- 6¾ ounces aged rum

Caramelized Pineapple:

- 1 pineapple (peeled, cored, cut into small cubes)
- 2 tbsp sugar cane syrup

Directions:

1. Add the raisins to a bowl, pour the rum over the raisins and allow to soak.

2. In the meantime, in a small bowl, dissolve the yeast in the warm water.

3. Mound the flour in a heap on a clean, work surface. Make a well in the middle of the flour.

4. Add the sugar, salt, 2 eggs, and the dissolved yeast into the well and with a wooden spoon, stir to form elastic dough.

5. Add another egg and mix thoroughly.

6. Finally, add the final egg along with 2¾ ounces of softened butter.

7. When the dough is elastic, add the soaked raisins and knead once more to combine.

8. Cover the dough with a clean tea towel and set aside to rise at room temperature for 60 minutes.

9. Using the remaining butter, grease 16 small rum baba molds.

10. Preheat the main oven to 480 degrees F.

11. When the dough is twice the size, evenly divide it between the 16 molds and bake in the preheated oven for 12 minutes.

12. Turn the babas out of the molds and set aside to cool.

13. To prepare the syrup: In a pan, boil the water with the sugar to form a thickened syrup.

14. Stir in the orange and lemon zest, along with the vanilla pod and rum.

15. Soak the babas in the hot syrup until bubbles are no longer rising to the top.

16. Remove and allow to drain on a wire baking rack.

17. In the meantime, prepare the caramelized pineapple.

18. Add the cubes of pineapple to the sugar syrup and over low heat, heat until they are saturated in syrup. When they are well coated, allow them to caramelize.

19. Serve the rum babas on individual dessert plates.

20. Arrange the caramelized pineapple cubes around the rum babas.

21. Serve and enjoy.

Gwyneth Paltrow: Five Spice Sweet Potato Muffins

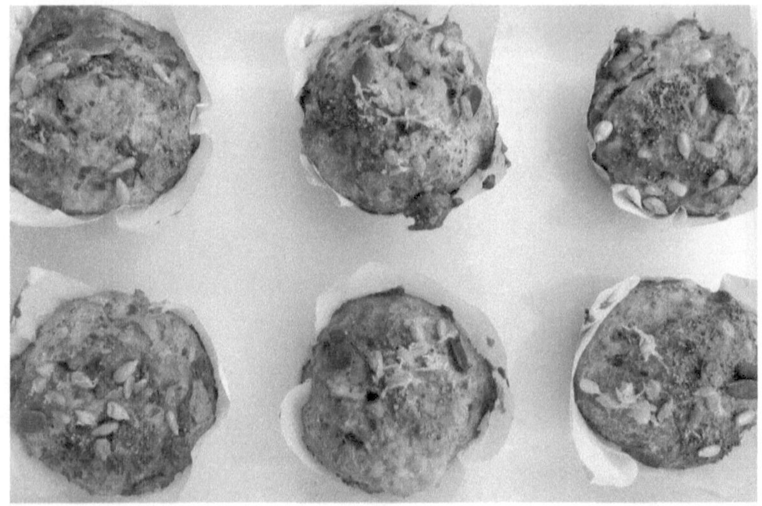

Award-winning actress, Gwyneth, loves experimenting with new flavors and these healthy, oriental-spiced muffins are no exception!

Servings: 12

Total Time: 1hour 30mins

Ingredients:

- Butter (to grease)
- 1 large sweet potato (priced with a fork)
- 4 ounces almond milk (unsweetened)
- 4 ounces good-quality olive oil
- 1 tsp vanilla essence
- 6 ounces + 2 tbsp maple syrup
- 2 tsp baking powder
- 1 pound 2 ounces gluten-free flour
- 1½ tsp Chinese 5-spice
- 2 tsp bicarb of soda
- ½ tsp sea salt

Directions:

1. Preheat the main oven to 400 degrees F. Grease a 12-hole muffin tin and set to one side.

2. Bake the potato in the oven for approximately an hour until soft. Allow to completely cool.

3. Peel the cool potato and mash using a fork.

4. Beat the milk, oil, vanilla essence, and 6 ounces of maple syrup into the potato until combined.

5. In a second bowl, combine the baking powder, flour, 5-spice, bicarb of soda, and salt.

6. Fold the dry mixture into the wet mixture until incorporated.

7. Spoon the batter into the muffin tin.

8. Place in the oven and bake for just over 20 minutes. For the last 5 minutes of baking brush the tops of the muffins with 2 tbsp maple syrup.

9. Allow to completely cool before serving.

Hugh Jackman: Banana Bread

Enjoy Hugh Jackman's moist banana bread with after-dinner coffee or tea.

Servings: 6-8

Total Time: 1hour 25mins

Ingredients:

- ½ cup butter (room temperature)
- 1 cup sugar
- 2 large eggs
- 1½ cups unbleached all-purpose flour
- 1 tsp baking soda
- 1 tsp kosher salt
- 1 cup very ripe bananas (mashed)
- ½ cup sour cream
- 1 tsp pure vanilla essence
- ½ cup pecans (chopped)

Directions:

1. Preheat the main oven to 350 degrees F. Using butter, lightly grease a 9x5x3" loaf pan and set to one side.

2. In an electric mixer, with a paddle, cream the butter with the sugar until fluffy.

3. Add the eggs, beating until entirely combined.

4. In a bowl, whisk the flour with the baking soda and salt.

5. Add to the butter mixture and mix until just incorporated.

6. Add the mashed bananas along with the sour cream and vanilla essence, mixing to combine.

7. Stir in the pecans and pour the mixture into the prepared pan.

8. Bake for approximately 1 hour 10 minutes until springy to the touch.

9. Turn the cake out onto a wire baking rack to cool.

Jamie Lee Curtis: Lemon Cake

Not only is Jamie Lee Curtis a successful award-winning actress but also she is the author of children's books. This recipe is her go-to lemon cake.

Servings: 16

Total Time:

Ingredients:

Cake:

- Nonstick vegetable baking spray
- Flour (to dust)
- 1 (18¼ ounce) yellow cake mix
- 1 (3 ounces) lemon gelatin
- ⅔ cup sunflower oil
- ⅔ cup hot water
- 4 large eggs

Glaze:

- 1 cup powdered sugar (sifted)
- 2 tbsp freshly squeezed lemon juice
- 1 tsp lemon zest (finely grated)

Directions:

1. Position a rack in the middle of the oven and preheat the main oven to 350 degrees F. Spritz a 12-cup Bundt pan with nonstick baking spray. Dust the pan lightly with flour, shaking off any excess flour put the pan to one side.

2. Add the yellow cake mix, gelatin, sunflower oil, hot water, and eggs to a mixing bowl and using an electric mixer, on low speed, beat for 60 seconds.

3. Turn the mixer off, and using a rubber spatula, scrape the sides of the bowl down.

4. Turn the mixer back on and set to moderate speed. Beat the mixture for 2 minutes, scraping the bowl down as necessary, until the batter is blended and thick.

5. Transfer the batter to the Bundt pan, smoothing and evening it out.

6. Place the pan in the oven and bake the cake for approximately 40 minutes, until light brown and beginning to pull away from the sides of the Bundt pan.

7. Remove the pan from the oven and transfer it to a wire baking rack for 10 minutes, to cool.

8. In the meantime, prepare the glaze: In a bowl, combine the powdered sugar with the freshly squeezed lemon juice and zest and using a wooden spoon, stir until silky smooth.

9. Take a long knife and run it around the edge of the cake, inverting it onto a cake platter.

10. Spoon the glaze over the still-warm cake allowing it to drip down.

11. Slice and serve.

Jane Fonda: Pumpkin Spice Bread

Jane Fonda a Golden Globe, Emmy, and Academy Award winner is also a political activist and fitness guru. This lightened-up pumpkin spice bread helps Jane stay trim and slim while satisfying those sweet cravings.

Servings: 8

Total Time: 1hour 30mins

Ingredients:

- Nonstick spray
- 2 tsp baking powder
- 2½ cups flour
- ¼ tsp nutmeg
- 1½ tsp cinnamon
- ¼ tsp cloves
- ¼ tsp salt
- ½ tsp bicarb of soda
- ½ cup brown sugar
- ¾ cup granulated sugar
- ¼ cup reduced fat margarine
- 2 eggs
- White of 1 egg
- 2 cups pureed pumpkin
- ⅓ cup + 2 tbsp fat-free plain yogurt

Directions:

1. Preheat the main oven to 350 degrees F. Spritz a regular-sized loaf tin with nonstick spray.

2. Combine the baking powder, flour, nutmeg, cinnamon, cloves, salt, and bicarb of soda in a bowl.

3. In a second bowl, beat together the sugars and margarine until creamy.

4. Next, beat in the eggs and white, followed by the pureed pumpkin and yogurt.

5. Fold the dry mixture into the wet mixture until incorporated.

6. Pour the batter into the loaf tin and bake for approximately an hour. Allow to cool completely before slicing and serving.

Jennifer Lawrence: Pecan Pie

Best known for her portrayal of Katniss Everdeen in the Hunger Games, this A-list superstar can't get enough of her Mom's pecan pie.

Servings: 8

Total Time: 1hour 20mins

Ingredients:

Light Corn Syrup Substitute:

- 2 cups white sugar
- ¾ cup water
- ¼ tsp cream of tartar
- Pinch of salt

Pie:

- 1 cup syrup
- 3 eggs (lightly beaten)
- ⅛ tsp salt
- 1 tsp vanilla essence
- ½ cup sugar
- 2 tbsp butter (melted)
- ½ cup pecans (chopped)
- ½ cup pecan halves
- 1 (9") unbaked pastry shell

Directions:

1. To prepare the syrup substitute: In a pan, combine the sugar with the water, cream of tartar and salt. Stir to combine and bring to boil.

2. Reduce the heat, cover with a lid and simmer for a few minutes.

3. Remove the lid and cook until the mixture reaches the soft ball stage, while frequently stirring.

4. Allow to cool and store at room temperature for up to 8 weeks.

5. For the pie: In a bowl, combine one cup of the prepared syrup with the beaten eggs, salt, vanilla essence, sugar, and butter.

6. Fold the pecans into the batter and pour the mixture into the unbaked pastry shell.

7. Transfer to an oven set at 400 degrees F for 15 minutes.

8. Turn the temperature down to 360 degrees F and bake for an additional 30-35 minutes, until the middle is slightly soft and the filling edges are firm.

9. Remove from the oven, allow to cool slightly and serve.

Joan Crawford: Fried Apple Rings

This leading lady's recipe for fried apple rings is sweet and simple and one the whole family can enjoy.

Servings: 4-6

Total Time: 10mins

Ingredients:

- 4 unpeeled, green apples (cored, sliced into thick rings)
- Freshly squeezed lemon juice
- ¼ pound butter
- Cinnamon (to dust)
- Nutmeg (to dust)
- Brown sugar (to serve)

Directions:

1. Add the slices of apples to a bowl and toss with lemon juice.

2. In a skillet, heat the butter.

3. When the butter is melted, in batches fry the apples until browned but not mushy. Flip over and repeat the process. This will only take 2-3 minutes.

4. Remove the apples from the pan and keep warm.

5. While the remaining slices of apple fry, sprinkle the top of the apples with cinnamon, nutmeg, and brown sugar.

Julia Roberts: Boozy Peach Pie

One of Hollywood's most prized actresses, mother of three and close friend to George Clooney, pretty woman Julia Roberts' dessert of choice is this peach cobbler-inspired dessert.

Servings: 12

Total Time: 1hour 10mins

Ingredients:

- 7 ripe, firm medium-size peaches (pitted, coarsely chopped)
- ¼ cup freshly squeezed lemon juice
- ¼ cup Scotch whiskey
- ¼ cup granulated sugar
- ¼ cup packed dark brown sugar
- 4 tbsp unsalted butter (chopped)

Topping:

- 2½ cups flour
- ½ cup packed dark brown sugar
- 1 tsp ground cinnamon
- 1½ cups unsalted butter (melted)
- Frozen vanilla yogurt (softened, to serve)

Directions:

1. Preheat the main oven to 350 degrees F. Butter a 13x9x2" casserole dish.

In a bowl, toss the peaches with the freshly squeezed lemon juice.

2. Add the Scotch whiskey along with the sugar, and brown sugar, and combine.

3. Spread the mixture onto the bottom of the dish and dot with small pieces of butter over the top.

4. For the topping: In a mixing bowl, stir the flour with the brown sugar, and cinnamon until incorporated.

5. Gradually add the butter while stirring to form a crumbly mixture. Sprinkle the mixture over the peaches to create a rustic look.

6. Cover the dish with aluminum foil and place in the preheated for 40 minutes.

7. Remove the foil and bake for between 5-10 minutes until browned on top.

Allow to cool slightly, before serving warm topped with scoops of softened frozen yogurt.

Katharine Hepburn: Brownies

This brownie recipe, just likes its creator, Katharine Hepburn, is a true classic that stands the test of time. Enjoy!

Servings: 16

Total Time: 45mins

Ingredients:

- ½ cup butter
- ½ cup cocoa
- 2 eggs
- 1 tsp vanilla essence
- 1 cup white sugar
- ¼ cup all-purpose flour
- 1 cup walnuts (chopped)
- Pinch of salt

Directions:

1. Preheat the main oven to 325 degrees F.

2. In a pan, melt the butter.

3. Add the cocoa to the melted butter and stir until entirely smooth.

4. Remove the pan from the heat and set aside to cool for 3 minutes.

5. Transfer the cooled mixture to a bowl and one at a time, whisk in the 2 eggs.

6. Stir in the vanilla essence to combine.

7. In a second bowl, combine the sugar with the flour, walnuts and a pinch of salt. Stir to combine and add to the cocoa mixture, stirring until just combined.

8. Transfer to an 8" square baking pan and bake in the oven for between 30-35 minutes. Take care not to over-bake as the brownies are ideally gooey.

9. Set aside to cool before cutting into bars.

Meryl Streep: Heart Cookies

Once the star of Julie & Julia and portraying the role of chef Julia Child, Meryl Streep is a passionate cook and home-maker.

Servings: 60

Total Time: 2hours 30mins

Ingredients:

- 1½ cups butter (softened)
- ¾ cup runny honey
- 1 tsp vanilla essence
- ⅔ cup almonds (finely ground)
- 1¾ cups whole wheat flour
- 1¾ cups all-purpose flour
- Jam (to fill, optional)

Directions:

1. In a bowl, using an electric mixer on moderate speed, cream the butter with the honey and vanilla essence.

2. Add the almonds, whole wheat flour, all-purpose flour, and mix until incorporated.

3. Divide the dough into 4 equal portions and wrap each one in kitchen wrap and transfer to the fridge for a minimum of 2 hours.

4. Preheat the main oven to 325 degrees F.

5. On a lightly floured sheet of wax paper, roll out 1 piece of dough to a ⅛" thickness.

6. Using a 3" heart-shaped cookie cutter, cut the dough into heart shapes. Wrap and refrigerate the dough trimmings.

7. Arrange the hearts on a cookie sheet.

8. Make a shallow thumbprint into the middle of each cookie and add a blob of jam into each indent.

9. Bake the cookies in the oven for between 12-15 minutes, until the edges are browned,

10. Allow the cookies to cool while still on the sheet for a couple of minutes, before transferring to a wire baking rack to completely cool.

11. Repeat the process with the remaining dough.

12. Enjoy.

Oprah Winfrey: Strawberry Sorbet

From the Color Purple to A Wrinkle in Time, this billionaire actress, talk show host, TV producer, and philanthropist, enjoys her desserts sweet and simple.

Servings: 8

Total Time: 6hours 15mins

Ingredients:

- 1 quart fresh strawberries (washed, hulled)
- ½ cup superfine sugar
- 1 tsp freshly squeezed lemon juice
- Pinch of fine sea salt.

Directions:

1. In a blender, combine the strawberries with the sugar, lemon juice, and salt and process until silky smooth.

2. Transfer the mixture to a container and place in the fridge for 2 hours, until cold.

3. Pour the mixture into your ice cream maker and churn according to the manufacturer's directions.

4. Serve and enjoy.

Tyra Banks: Old Fashioned Coffee Cake

Model, celebrity and actress, Tyra Banks' family coffee cake recipe is a true tea-time classic.

Servings: 12-16

Total Time: 1hour 5mins

Ingredients:

- 4 cups all-purpose flour
- 2 cups packed brown sugar
- 1 cup granulated sugar
- 1½ tsp salt
- 1 tsp nutmeg
- 1¼ cups vegetable oil
- 2 tsp baking powder
- 1 tsp baking soda
- 3 eggs
- 1½ cups buttermilk
- 2 tsp cinnamon

Directions:

1. Preheat the main oven to 350 degrees F.

2. In a bowl, combine the flour with the brown sugar, granulated sugar, salt, and nutmeg until lump-free.

3. Stir in the oil, setting aside 1½ cups of the mixture to use for topping. Set to one side.

4. Into the bowl, stir in the baking powder, soda along with the eggs, buttermilk, and cinnamon.

5. Spread the batter into a greased 13x9" baking pan.

6. Scatter the topping over the top and bake in the oven for 45 minutes, until springy to the touch.

Vincent Price: Cheesecake

King of horror, Vincent Price, together with his wife Mary, held lots of lavish dinner parties at their Beverly Hills mansion. The actor loved food, and in 1965, he and Mary even wrote a cookery book!

Servings: 6-8

Total Time: 8hours 20mins

Ingredients:

Butter:

- Graham cracker crumbs
- 12 ounces cream cheese (softened)
- ¾ cup sugar
- 4 egg yolks
- 2 tbsp flour
- 1½ tsp vanilla essence
- ½ tsp salt
- 4 egg whites
- 2 cups light cream (scalded)
- Strawberries (washed, hulled, to serve, optional)

Directions:

1. Using butter, grease an 8" springform pan. Turn the pan on its side and sprinkle over some cracker crumbs and lightly shake so they stick to the sides.

2. When the sides are well and evenly coated, shake a light cracker crumb coating onto the bottom of the pan.

3. Transfer the pan to the fridge for 2 hours, or to the freezer for half an hour.

4. Using an electric mixer, combine the cream cheese with the sugar, egg yolks, flour, vanilla essence, and salt. Beat until the mixture is silky smooth. Reduce the speed to low and a little at a time, pour in the scaled light cream.

5. Preheat the main oven to 300 degrees F.

6. Beat the whites until stiff but not dry and add them to the cream cheese mixture, folding in well but lightly.

7. Transfer the mixture to the prepared springform pan and set the pan in a shallow baking pan containing 1" of hot water.

8. Bake in the preheated oven for 90 minutes.

9. Place the cheesecake in the fridge for a minimum of 6 hours before serving.

10. Serve, covered with a layer of fresh strawberries.

About the Author

Born in New Germantown, Pennsylvania, Stephanie Sharp received a Masters degree from Penn State in English Literature. Driven by her passion to create culinary masterpieces, she applied and was accepted to The International Culinary School of the Art Institute where she excelled in French cuisine. She has married her cooking skills with an aptitude for business by opening her own small cooking school where she teaches students of all ages.

Stephanie's talents extend to being an author as well and she has written over 400 e-books on the art of cooking and baking that include her most popular recipes.

Sharp has been fortunate enough to raise a family near her hometown in Pennsylvania where she, her husband and children live in a beautiful rustic house on an extensive piece of land. Her other passion is taking care of the furry members of her family which include 3 cats, 2 dogs and a potbelly pig named Wilbur.

Watch for more amazing books by Stephanie Sharp coming out in the next few months.

Author's Afterthoughts

I am truly grateful to you for taking the time to read my book. I cherish all of my readers! Thanks ever so much to each of my cherished readers for investing the time to read this book!

With so many options available to you, your choice to buy my book is an honour, so my heartfelt thanks at reading it from beginning to end!

I value your feedback, so please take a moment to submit an honest and open review on Amazon so I can get valuable insight into my readers' opinions and others can benefit from your experience.

Thank you for taking the time to review!

Stephanie Sharp

For announcements about new releases, please follow my author page on Amazon.com!

(Look for the Follow Bottom under the photo)

You can find that at:

https://www.amazon.com/author/stephanie-sharp

*or Scan **QR-code** below.*